# Bánh Mì

## Vietnamese Sandwich Guide

Essential Recipe Handbook for the Authentic
Craft of Delicious Mouth Watering Homemade
Vietnamese Culture

Nancy Nguyen

# Legal

---

**NOTE:** Some of the recipes in this book include raw eggs. Raw eggs may contain bacteria. It is recommended that you purchase certified salmonella-free eggs from a reliable source and store them in the refrigerator. You should not feed raw eggs to babies or small kids. Likewise, pregnant women, elderly persons, or those with a compromised immune system should not eat raw eggs. Neither the author nor the publisher claims responsibility for adverse effects resulting from the use of the recipes and/or information found within this book.

---

# Introduction

## Finger Lickin' DELICIOUSNESS!

This Vietnamese traditional sandwich will be the best addition to your food arsenal and your friends and family will be thanking you for bringing it into your home. Everyone loves a sandwich, but to fly it in from the Vietnamese culture will be a real treat. You will soon learn the art and craft of the delicacy! The Sandwich Professional is what your new title will be in the realm of your very own kitchen.

This very popular sandwich is "for sure" a mouth waterer. For many years many have tried but most have not succeeded in this craft. We have brought to you a very special and creative handbook to give you the skills to "Master the Craft."

Get ready to invite your family and friends over for some delicious, exciting, tongue twisting and mouth-watering fulfillment, to say the least. Mastering the craft of the pickling and carving the vegetable is the secret to getting it done the right way. So, sit back and turn the pages and "Dive Into some of these hunger busting meals. You will start to create your very own Bánh Mì Creations. Remember...these sandwiches are a craft, so the only one who will know these secrets is you!

Enjoy!

# Table of Contents

Legal ........................................... 1

Introduction ............................... 3
Finger Lickin' DELICIOUSNESS! ....... 3

Table of Contents ...................... 4

Chapter 1: What is a Bánh Mì? ..... 5
Bánh Mì, Pronounced [Bon-Mee] ..... 5

Chapter 2: The Art and Craft of the
Bánh Mì Sandwich ...................... 6
How to Make a Bánh Mì Like a Pro ... 6

Chapter 3: Types of Bread to Use .... 7
It's All About the Bread ............... 7

Chapter 4: Sauces & Condiments .... 8
The Process of the Pickles ............ 8
Pickled Carrots & Daikons, Secret
Condiments ............................. 9
Secret Banh Mi Mayonnaise ......... 10
Ingredients to Have On Hand ....... 11
Before You Go Further! ............... 12

Chapter 5: The Sandwich Selections 13

Pork ........................................ 14
Bánh Mì Dac Biet ( The Classic Banh Mi) 14
Bánh Mì Pate Saigon .................. 16
Bánh Mì Pate Cha Lua ................ 18
Bánh Mì Pate Thit Nguoi ............. 20
Bánh Mì Dac Biet (The Classic Banh Mi) 22
Bánh Mì Bi ............................... 24
Bánh Mì Thit Nuon .................... 26
Bánh Mì Nem Nuong .................. 28
Bánh Mì Xui Mai ....................... 30

Beef ........................................ 32
Banh Thit Bo Nuong .................. 32
Grilled Steak Bánh Mì ................ 34
Brisket Bánh Mì ........................ 36
Roast Beef Bánh Mì ................... 37
Red Curry Ground Beef Bánh Mì .... 39

Poultry .................................... 41
Banh Ga Nuong ........................ 41
Thanksgiving Turkey Bánh Mì ....... 43
Southwestern Turkey Bánh Mì ...... 45
Pesto Turkey Bánh Mì ................ 47
Spicy Crispy Chicken Bánh Mì ...... 49

Vegetarian ............................... 51
Bánh Mì Chay ........................... 51
Vegan Beef Lemongrass Banh Mi .... 53
Spicy Ginger Eggplant Banh Mi ..... 55
Ginger Lemongrass Portobello Mushroom
Banh Mi ................................... 57
Grilled Vegetable Banh Mi ........... 59

Fish ......................................... 61
Bánh Mì Ca Moi ........................ 61
Salmon Banh Mi ........................ 63
Soft Shell Crab Banh Mi .............. 65
Fried Oyster Banh Mi ................. 67
Coconut Shrimp Banh Mi ............ 69
Lobster Roll Banh Mi .................. 71

Next On the List! ....................... 73
Here's What You Do Now... ......... 73
Yours to Keep! .......................... 74
About The Author ...................... 75
Personal Bánh Mì Recipes & Notes: .. 76

# Chapter 1:
# What is a Bánh Mì?

## Bánh Mì, Pronounced [Bon-Mee]

Let's start with what Bánh Mì means. Bánh in Vietnamese refers to multiple different kinds of food including bread and Mi translates to wheat. The combination means bread but for this sandwich it's specifically a Vietnamese baguette. The Vietnamese baguette is airier than others and has a soft, chewy texture on the insides. A Traditional Bánh Mì uses a single serving size baguette that's filled with roasted pork, pork pate, pickled vegetables, cilantro, jalapeños, and mayonnaise. The sandwich contains cucumbers, carrots, and daikon radish. The sandwich has a great crunch thanks to the crusty bread and pickled veggies.

# Chapter 2:
# The Art and Craft of the Bánh Mì Sandwich

## How to Make a Bánh Mì Like a Pro

Part of what makes a Bánh Mì so great is how it's prepared. Make sure you use fresh bread so it's nice and crunchy. The cucumber should either be a thick spear or thinly sliced. The radish and carrots should be julienned so they're matchstick size. Always slice the jalapeño thin as well. The order of the ingredients is hugely important.

Start by cutting the baguette in half lengthwise and spreading mayonnaise on both pieces. You want to place a nice thick layer of pork pate on the bottom piece of baguette. Top that with the cucumber and then a layer of the pickled carrots and radish. Top the pickles with the roast pork, cilantro and add as much jalapeño as you'd like and put the top piece of bread on the jalapenos. Then take a bite of this mouthwatering, delicious sandwich.

# Chapter 3:
# Types of Bread to Use

## It's All About the Bread

Ideally you want to use a Vietnamese baguette when making the sandwich. The use of rice flour in the baguette gives the bread an airy texture and crunchy crust. Go to a Vietnamese bakery if you can to pick some up. You can also try asking your local Vietnamese restaurant if they'll see you some. Otherwise use a fresh French baguette from your local bakery. As the sandwiches has made its way around the world people have started making variations with all different types of bread. Some people have even used croissants to make them. If you want that classic, crunchy sandwich stick with either a Vietnamese or French baguette.

# Chapter 4:
# Sauces & Condiments

## The Process of the Pickles

Pickles are an essential part of a Bánh Mì and Asian cuisine in general. Most people don't have time to wait around for vegetables to pickle because traditional pickles take a couple days. This pickle recipe is ready in as little as an hour. If you want a more intense flavor let the pickles marinate longer. Although daikon radish and carrots are used in this recipe you can swap in any vegetable. Always cut the vegetables thinly to better absorb the marinade.

# Pickled Carrots & Daikon's, Secret Condiments

Prep Time: 5 Minutes
Cook Time: 20 Minutes
Servings: About 3 cup

## INGREDIENTS:
*1 ½ large carrots, peeled and cut into thick matchsticks*
*¾ pound daikon, each no larger than 2 inches in diameter, peeled and cut into thick matchsticks*
*1 teaspoon salt*
*2 teaspoons plus 1/2 cup sugar*
*1 1/4 cups distilled white vinegar*
*1 cup lukewarm water*

## DIRECTIONS:
> Put the vegetables in a bowl and season with the salt and 2 teaspoons of sugar. Knead the vegetables for 3 minutes using your hands. This will get the water out of the vegetables. You should stop when the daikon is flexible enough to touch tips without breaking. Use a colander to drain the vegetable and rinse them with cold water. Gently press out the excess water after rinsing. Place the vegetables in bowl if you're planning on using the pickles right away or in a re-sealable jar for later use.

> Mix the water, vinegar and remaining ½ cup of sugar until the sugar dissolves. Pour the liquid over the vegetables and cover the bowl or jar. Let the vegetables marinate in the brine for at least an hour.

> The vegetable will keep fresh in the refrigerator for up to 4 weeks.

# Secret Bánh Mì Mayonnaise

Prep Time: 5 Minutes
Servings:  About 1/2 cup

## INGREDIENTS:

*1 egg yolk*
*1/2 cup oil (canola or corn)*
*1 pinch of kosher salt*
*1 teaspoon fresh lemon juice*
*1 clove finely minced garlic (optional)*
*1 teaspoon Sriracha Sause (is you like a little kick to your sandwiches! (optional)*

## DIRECTIONS:

> Whisk egg yolk, salt, and lemon juice with 2 tablespoons of oil, garlic & Sriracha sauce in a large mixing bowl. (garlic/Sriracha optional)
> Whisk til ingredients are emulsified.
> Next, drizzle the remaining oil slowly
> Continue to whisk until mixture becomes like a creamy consistency.

**Alternate Method:**
> Place all ingredients in a blender and slowly mix in the oil while blending until it turns creamy. Make final adjustment with seasoning.

**If you're really want to spice things up:**
For a little bit of a different twist, it's OK to add different seasonings. Some alternatives can be...garlic, Sriracha, mustard, chipotle, roasted red peppers, Creole seasoning, ginger, sesame oil, even wasabi powder.
**Make it your own creation!**

# Ingredients to Have on Hand

Ingredients in a Bánh Mì can vary slightly from city to city and food cart to food cart. Below is a list of the typical ingredients you might find in traditional Bánh Mì variations.

1.  Pickled Carrots

2.  Pickled Radishes

3.  Cucumbers or pickled cucumbers

4.  Fish sauce *(optional)*

5.  Mayonnaise

6.  Jalapeños

7.  Cilantro

8.  Basil

9.  Mint

10. Soy sauce or Maggi seasoning sauce.

11. Sriracha Sause of you like a little kick to your sandwiches! *(optional)*

## Before You Go Further!

# GET YOUR FREE GUIDE TODAY!

**Steps to Making the Perfect Home Made Vietnamese Craft Bánh Mì Sandwich!** This quick start guide will show you the way to get the **BEST Bánh Mì sandwich made fast!** This **QUICK STEP GUIDE** will make you a pro at crafting those sandwich, and your friends and family will love you for it! Simply click the button below! Enjoy your Bánh Mì Vietnamese Sandwich Experience! **GET YOURS NOW!**

http://eepurl.com/dvHwST

# Chapter 5:
# The Sandwich Selections

# Pork

## Bánh Mì Dac Biet ( The Classic Banh Mi)

This is the classic Bánh Mì sandwich that you've heard so much about. It's a mixture of textures, as well as flavors including, sweet, savory, and spicy

Prep Time: 1 hour 10 Minutes
Cook Time: 20 Minutes
Servings: 4

### INGREDIENTS:
*1 pound mix of pickled daikon radish and carrots*
*1 pound pork tenderloin*
*1 ½ teaspoons sugar*
*½ teaspoon salt*
*3 tablespoons chili garlic sauce*
*8-12 sprigs of cilantro*
*8 ounces pork pate*
*16 thinly sliced cucumber strips or spears*
*4 7-inch Vietnamese baguettes*
*1 jar mayonnaise*
*A few thinly sliced jalapenos, to taste*

### DIRECTIONS:
> Preheat your oven to 400F.
> Mix together the chili sauce and sugar. Coat the pork with the mixture. Sprinkle the salt all over the pork.
> Transfer the pork to the rack of a roasting pan that's been sprayed with cooking spray. Cook the pork in the oven for about 20 minutes, until it's a little pink on the inside. Allow the pork to cool for a little then cover it and place it in the refrigerator.

> When the pork is cold slice it thinly.
> Preheat oven to 325F.
> Cut the baguettes lengthwise and spread mayonnaise on the cut side of each piece. Place them in the oven for a couple minutes. Allow the hot toasted bread to cool slightly.
> Spread an even amount of pate on the bottoms pieces of all 4 baguettes. Top with 4 pieces of cucumber and an even amount of pickles. Place an even amount of pork on top of the pickles. Add 2 to 3 sprigs of cilantro on top of the pork and your desired amount of jalapenos.
> Top with the other piece of baguette and serve immediately.

# Bánh Mì Pate Saigon

This is just like the classic Bánh Mì but made with pork belly. Pork belly is a fattier cut of meat that's full of flavor. You get a nice taste of pork in this sandwich.

Prep Time: 5 Minutes
Cook Time: 20 Minutes
Servings: 4

## INGREDIENTS:
*1 pound mix of pickled daikon radish and carrots*
*1 pound cooked pork belly*
*½ cup soy sauce*
*8-12 sprigs of cilantro*
*8 ounces pork pate*
*16 thinly sliced cucumber strips or spears*
*4 7-inch Vietnamese baguettes*
*1 jar mayonnaise*
*A few thinly sliced jalapenos, to taste*

## DIRECTIONS:
> Preheat your oven to 320F.
> Put the pork belly on a lined baking sheet and drizzle the soy sauce on top.
> Cook the pork in the oven for about 20 minutes, until it's roasted. Allow to cool slightly before slicing it thinly.
> Heat the oven to 325F.
> Cut the baguettes lengthwise and spread mayonnaise on the cut side of each piece. Place them in the oven for a couple minutes. Allow the hot toasted bread to cool slightly.
> Spread an even amount of pate on the bottoms pieces of all 4 baguettes. Top with 4 pieces of cucumber and an even amount of

pickles. Place an even amount of pork on top of the pickles. Add 2 to 3 sprigs of cilantro on top of the pork and your desired amount of jalapenos.

> Top with the other piece of baguette and serve immediately.

# Bánh Mì Pate Cha Lua

Cha Lua is a steamed Vietnamese pork loaf. It's mildly flavored which allows all the ingredients in the sandwich to work in harmony.

Prep Time: 3 hours 30 Minutes
Cook Time: 20-25 Minutes
Servings: 4

## INGREDIENTS:
### Pork:
*2 pounds Ground Pork*
*2 tablespoons Fish Sauce*
*2 tablespoons Sugar*
*1/2 teaspoon Salt*
*1 teaspoon fresh Ground Pepper*
*1 Shallot, minced*
*2 cloves Garlic, minced*
*1/4 cup ice water*
*2 tablespoons Tapioca Flour*
*1 bag Alsa Baking Powder or any single action Baking Powder brand (2 teaspoons)*
*1 teaspoon Peppercorns*
*Banana Leaves, rinsed and pat dried*
*Twine, to tie*

*1 pound mix of pickled daikon radish and carrots*
*8-12 sprigs of cilantro*
*8 ounces pork pate*
*16 thinly sliced cucumber strips or spears*
*4 7-inch Vietnamese baguettes*
*1 jar mayonnaise*
*A few thinly sliced jalapenos, to taste*

## DIRECTIONS:

> Mix the first 7 ingredients in a bowl. Combine the water and tapioca in a separate bowl. Make sure there's a lot of room in the bowl. Mix the baking powder into tapioca mixture. The mixture will expand because of the baking powder. Pour the tapioca mixture into the pork mixture and combine the two.

> Cover the new mixture and freeze for about 3 hours. The mixture should be very cold but not frozen.

> Turn the mixture into a paste by processing it in a food processor. Divide the pork into 2 equal sized batches. Process the batches one at a time until smooth. Then mix in the peppercorns.

> Form the paste into a log on the banana leaves. Brush your hands and the banana leaves with cooking oil so the paste doesn't stick to either. Wrap the log in at least 3 layers of banana leaves. Make sure to fold two ends of the banana leaves and tie the twine around it tightly to secure it.

> Steam the pork mixture for about 20-25 minutes, until cooked through. Allow to cool slightly before slicing it thinly.

> Heat the oven to 325F.

> Cut the baguettes lengthwise and spread mayonnaise on the cut side of each piece. Place them in the oven for a couple minutes. Allow the hot toasted bread to cool slightly.

> Spread an even amount of pate on the bottoms pieces of all 4 baguettes. Top with 4 pieces of cucumber and an even amount of pickles. Place an even amount of pork on top of the pickles. Add 2 to 3 sprigs of cilantro on top of the pork and your desired amount of jalapenos.

> Top with the other piece of baguette and serve immediately.

# Bánh Mì Pate Thit Nguoi

This version of the classic sandwich uses cold cuts. In our recipe, we use headcheese and ham which you should be able to find at your local deli. You can always swap in your favorite pork cold cuts.

Prep Time: 7 Minutes
Cook Time: 2 Minutes
Servings: 4

## INGREDIENTS:
*1 pound mix of pickled daikon radish and carrots*
*½ pound thinly sliced headcheese*
*½ pound thinly sliced ham*
*1 ½ teaspoons sugar*
*½ teaspoon salt*
*3 tablespoons chili garlic sauce*
*8-12 sprigs of cilantro*
*8 ounces pork pate*
*16 thinly sliced cucumber strips or spears*
*4 7-inch Vietnamese baguettes*
*1 jar mayonnaise*
*A few thinly sliced jalapenos, to taste*

## DIRECTIONS:
> Preheat oven to 325F.
> Cut the baguettes lengthwise and spread mayonnaise on the cut side of each piece. Place them in the oven for a couple minutes. Allow the hot toasted bread to cool slightly.
> Spread an even amount of pate on the bottoms pieces of all 4 baguettes. Top with 4 pieces of cucumber and an even amount of pickles. Place an even amount of pork and headcheese on top of the

pickles. Add 2 to 3 sprigs of cilantro on top of the pork and your desired amount of jalapenos.

> Top with the other piece of baguette and serve immediately.

# Bánh Mì Dac Biet (The Classic Banh Mi)

This is the classic Bánh Mì sandwich that you've heard so much about. It's a mixture of textures, as well as flavors including, sweet, savory, and spicy

Prep Time: 1 hour 10 Minutes
Cook Time: 20 Minutes
Servings: 4

## INGREDIENTS:

*1 pound mix of pickled daikon radish and carrots*
*1 pound pork tenderloin*
*1 ½ teaspoons sugar*
*½ teaspoon salt*
*3 tablespoons chili garlic sauce*
*8-12 sprigs of cilantro*
*8 ounces pork pate*
*16 thinly sliced cucumber strips or spears*
*4 7-inch Vietnamese baguettes*
*1 jar mayonnaise*
*A few thinly sliced jalapenos, to taste*

## DIRECTIONS:

> Preheat your oven to 400F.
> Mix together the chili sauce and sugar. Coat the pork with the mixture. Sprinkle the salt all over the pork.
> Transfer the pork to the rack of a roasting pan that's been sprayed with cooking spray. Cook the pork in the oven for about 20 minutes, until it's a little pink on the inside. Allow the pork to cool for a little then cover it and place it in the refrigerator.
> When the pork is cold slice it thinly.
> Preheat oven to 325F.

> Cut the baguettes lengthwise and spread mayonnaise on the cut side of each piece. Place them in the oven for a couple minutes. Allow the hot toasted bread to cool slightly.

> Spread an even amount of pate on the bottoms pieces of all 4 baguettes. Top with 4 pieces of cucumber and an even amount of pickles. Place an even amount of pork on top of the pickles. Add 2 to 3 sprigs of cilantro on top of the pork and your desired amount of jalapenos.

> Top with the other piece of baguette and serve immediately.

# Bánh Mì Bi

This Bánh Mì features shredded pork and pork skin. Pork skin is used in a lot of different cuisine and is usually fried. Not in this dish, it's served simply with rice powder, salt, white pepper, and garlic powder.

Prep Time: 20 Minutes
Cook Time: 20 Minutes
Servings: 4

## INGREDIENTS:
*1 pound mix of pickled daikon radish and carrots*
*1 package pork skin*
*½ pound pork cutlet*
*4 tablespoons soy sauce*
*4 tablespoons roasted rice powder*
*1 teaspoon garlic powder*
*Fresh ground white pepper*
*1 tablespoon olive oil*
*1 tablespoon sugar*
*1 teaspoon salt*
*8-12 sprigs of cilantro*
*8 ounces pork pate*
*16 thinly sliced cucumber strips or spears*
*4 7-inch Vietnamese baguettes*
*1 jar mayonnaise*
*A few thinly sliced jalapenos, to taste*

## DIRECTIONS:
❯ Use the salt to coat the pork skin. Then rinse the skin with room temperature water. Continue to wash until the skin no longer feels fatty. Drain the skins and dry them completely.

> Heat the oil in a sauté pan on medium heat. Once it's hot add in the pork cutlet, sugar and soy sauce. Cook for roughly 20 minutes.
> Cut the pork cutlet into matchstick size pieces and cut the pork skin into 1 inch pieces.
> Mix the pork skin with the rice powder, garlic powder and add salt and white pepper to taste.
> Mix the pork skin and cutlet together.
> Cut the baguettes lengthwise and spread mayonnaise on the cut side of each piece. Place them in the oven for a couple minutes. Allow the hot toasted bread to cool slightly.
> Spread an even amount of pate on the bottoms pieces of all 4 baguettes. Top with 4 pieces of cucumber and an even amount of pickles. Place an even amount of pork on top of the pickles. Add 2 to 3 sprigs of cilantro on top of the pork and your desired amount of jalapenos.
> Top with the other piece of baguette and serve immediately.

# Bánh Mì Thit Nuon

This is the classic Bánh Mì sandwich that you've heard so much about. It's a mixture of textures, as well as flavors including, sweet, savory, and spicy

Prep Time: 1 hour 10 Minutes
Cook Time: 15 Minutes
Servings: 4

## INGREDIENTS:

*1/4 cup minced Lemongrass*
*1/4 cup sugar*
*2 tablespoons fish sauce*
*1 tablespoon ground pepper*
*1-2 cloves garlic, minced.*
*2-3 shallots, minced.*
*3 tablespoons sesame oil*
*1 tablespoon thick soy sauce*
*1 pound mix of pickled daikon radish and carrots*
*1.5 lb. pork butt or shoulder, thinly sliced just under 1/4 inch*
*8-12 sprigs of cilantro*
*8 ounces pork pate*
*16 thinly sliced cucumber strips or spears*
*4 7-inch Vietnamese baguettes*
*1 jar mayonnaise*
*A few thinly sliced jalapenos, to taste*

## DIRECTIONS:

> Combine the first 8 ingredients in a large bowl and then add in the pork. Allow the pork to marinate at least an hour.
> Preheat your grill to medium heat.
> Grill the pork for about 6 minutes a side until it's golden brown with a slight char.

> Cut the pork into 4 equal portions.
> Cut the baguettes lengthwise and spread mayonnaise on the cut side of each piece. Place them in the oven for a couple minutes. Allow the hot toasted bread to cool slightly.
> Spread an even amount of pate on the bottoms pieces of all 4 baguettes. Top with 4 pieces of cucumber and an even amount of pickles. Place an even amount of pork on top of the pickles. Add 2 to 3 sprigs of cilantro on top of the pork and your desired amount of jalapenos.
> Top with the other piece of baguette and serve immediately.

# Bánh Mì Nem Nuong

This version of the sandwich is made with homemade Vietnamese sausage. It has a lovely aromatic flavor that you won't get enough of.

Prep Time: 1 hour 15 Minutes
Cook Time: 10 Minutes
Servings: 4

## INGREDIENTS:

*2 lbs. ground pork with at least 20% fat*
*1/4 cup granulated white sugar*
*1/4 cup fish sauce*
*1 tablespoon minced garlic*
*1 tablespoon roasted rice powder*
*3 tablespoons Tusino Nem Nuong curing powder*
*1 pound mix of pickled daikon radish and carrots*
*8-12 sprigs of cilantro*
*8 ounces pork pate*
*16 thinly sliced cucumber strips or spears*
*4 7-inch Vietnamese baguettes*
*1 jar mayonnaise*
*A few thinly sliced jalapenos, to taste*

## DIRECTIONS:

❯ Combine the first 6 ingredients in a large bowl. Allow the pork mixture to refrigerate for at least an hour.
❯ Oil up your hands and form the meat into balls or patties.
❯ Preheat your grill to medium heat.
❯ Grill the pork for about 7-10 minutes a side until completely cooked.
❯ Cut the baguettes lengthwise and spread mayonnaise on the cut side of each piece. Place them in the oven for a couple minutes. Allow the hot toasted bread to cool slightly.

> Spread an even amount of pate on the bottoms pieces of all 4 baguettes. Top with 4 pieces of cucumber and an even amount of pickles. Place an even amount of pork on top of the pickles. Add 2 to 3 sprigs of cilantro on top of the pork and your desired amount of jalapenos.
> Top with the other piece of baguette and serve immediately.

# Bánh Mì Xui Mai

This version of the sandwich is made with homemade meatballs. It has a delicious Vietnamese tomato sauce that includes soy sauce, sugar and garlic. You'll never look at a meatball sandwich the same way.

Prep Time: 20 Minutes
Cook Time: 30 Minutes
Servings: 4

## INGREDIENTS:

*Meatballs:*
1 pound ground pork
1 large egg
3 cloves garlic, minced
½ cup minced green onion
½ cup minced jicama
½ tablespoon cornstarch
½ tablespoon Wondra flour
½ tablespoon fish sauce
½ tablespoon soy sauce
½ tablespoon sugar
½ teaspoon salt

*Sauce:*
½ cup water
½ tablespoon cornstarch
½ tablespoon sugar
½ tablespoon soy sauce
½ teaspoon salt
8 ounces canned tomato sauce
1 tablespoons canola oil

1 cloves garlic, minced
½ tablespoon sugar
1 scallion, chopped
½ teaspoon black pepper
Light sprinkling of garlic powder
Light sprinkling of onion powder
Light sprinkling of ginger powder

1 pound mix of pickled daikon radish and carrots
8-12 sprigs of cilantro
4 7-inch Vietnamese baguettes

## DIRECTIONS:

> Mix all the meatball ingredients in a bowl using your hands. Form the combined mixture into 1 inch meatballs

> Steam the meatballs for 20-30 minutes, until cooked through.

> While the meatballs are steaming, mix together the tomato sauce, corn starch, water, sugar, soy sauce, and salt.

> Heat the oil in a small saucepan on high heat. Put in the garlic and allow it to cook for 30 seconds. Add in the corn starch mixture and stir everything until the sauce thickens.

> Cut the baguettes lengthwise. Place them in the oven for a couple minutes. Allow the hot toasted bread to cool slightly.

> Cut the meatballs in half and place an equal amount in the baguettes. Pour sauce over the meatballs. Top with an even amount of pickles. Add 2 to 3 sprigs of cilantro on top of the pickles.

> Top with the other piece of baguette and serve immediately.

# Beef

## Banh Thit Bo Nuong

This classic feature ground beef patties that are flavored with lemongrass and garlic. The lemongrass and garlic add a lovely aromatic flavor that blends perfectly with the pickles.

Prep Time: 45 Minutes
Cook Time: 20 Minutes
Servings: 4

### INGREDIENTS:
*1 lb. of 80/20 ground beef*
*1 large white or yellow onion, finely chopped*
*4 tablespoons of finely minced lemongrass*
*3 tablespoon of hoisin sauce*
*5 cloves of garlic, minced*
*3 tsp sugar*
*1 tsp five spices*
*3 tablespoon canola oil*
*2 tablespoon fish sauce*
*1/2 tsp salt*

### For the sauce:
*2 tablespoon of hoisin sauce*
*1/4 cup of juice from the grilled beef if grilled in the oven or beef broth if grilling the meat*
*1 tsp of sugar, black pepper*

*1 pound mix of pickled daikon radish and carrots*
*8-12 sprigs of cilantro*

*16 thinly sliced cucumber strips or spears*
*4 7-inch Vietnamese baguettes*
*1 jar mayonnaise*
*A few thinly sliced jalapenos, to taste*

## DIRECTIONS:

> Mix the first 10 ingredients together in a bowl. Allow the mixture to marinate for 15 minutes, and then create 2 inch patties out of it.
> Preheat oven to 400F if using the oven or preheat the grill to medium heat.
> If cooking in the oven, line a tray with aluminum foil and place the patties on it. Cook in the oven for 20 minutes. Flip the patties occasionally. At the 15 minute mark drain the juices from the tray into a bowl and drizzle the patties with a little oil. Cook for 5 more minutes. If grilling, grill the patties for about 5 minutes per side.
> Place all the sauce ingredient in a pan and heat on high heat until it's bubbling. Then turn off the heat. Allow it cool off until it reaches room temperature.
> Cut the baguettes lengthwise and spread mayonnaise on the cut side of each piece. Place them in the oven for a couple minutes. Allow the hot toasted bread to cool slightly.
> Drizzle the bottom piece with a teaspoon of the sauce and top with 4 pieces of cucumber and an even amount of pickles. Place an even amount of beef on top of the pickles. Add 2 to 3 sprigs of cilantro on top of the beef drizzle with a 2nd teaspoon of sauce and top with your desired amount of jalapenos.
> Top with the other piece of baguette and serve immediately.

# Grilled Steak Bánh Mì

A little grilled steak lives up this sandwich and will have you asking for more. The basil adds the perfect complement to the flavor of the steak

Prep Time: 1 hour 10 Minutes
Cook Time: 6 Minutes
Servings: 4

## INGREDIENTS:
*3 tablespoons fish sauce*
*4 tablespoons sugar*
*2 tablespoons finely minced shallot*
*6 cloves of garlic, minced*
*1/2 teaspoon ground black pepper*
*1 pound beef sirloin tip, sliced into 1/8-inch strips*
*1 pound mix of pickled daikon radish and carrots*
*8-12 sprigs of basil*
*16 thinly sliced cucumber strips or spears*
*4 7-inch Vietnamese baguettes*
*1 jar mayonnaise*
*A few thinly sliced jalapenos, to taste*

## DIRECTIONS:
> Whisk together the first 5 ingredients in a small bowl and then place it in a re-sealable plastic bag along with the beef. Allow the beef to marinate at least an hour and up to 24 hours in the refrigerator.
> Preheat your grill to high heat.
> Grill the beef for about 2-3 minutes a side until fully cooked.
> Cut the baguettes lengthwise and spread mayonnaise on the cut side of each piece. Place them in the oven for a couple minutes. Allow the hot toasted bread to cool slightly.

> Top with 4 pieces of cucumber and an even amount of pickles. Place an even amount of beef on top of the pickles. Add 2 to 3 sprigs of basil on top of the beef and your desired amount of jalapenos.
> Top with the other piece of baguette and serve immediately.

# Brisket Bánh Mì

This sandwich is filled with all types of delicious flavor. The mayonnaise has been switched out for a BBQ aioli to complement the brisket, and the jalapenos for pickled Fresno chilies for some tangy heat.

Prep Time:  40 Minutes
Cook Time: 2 Minutes
Servings: 4

## INGREDIENTS:
*1 cup of mayonnaise*
*1/4 cup of your favorite BBQ sauce*
*3 teaspoons of Apple Cider Vinegar*
*1 1/2 teaspoon of Cajun Seasoning*
*1/4 teaspoon garlic powder*
*1 pound thinly sliced brisket*
*1 pound mix of pickled daikon radish and carrots*
*8-12 sprigs of cilantro*
*16 thinly sliced cucumbers strips or spears*
*4 7-inch Vietnamese baguettes*
*A few thinly sliced pickled Fresno chilies, to taste*

## DIRECTIONS:
> Mix together the first 5 ingredients in a bowl and then chill for 30 minutes in the refrigerator, covered.
> Cut the baguettes lengthwise and spread aioli on the cut side of each piece. Place them in the oven for a couple minutes. Allow the hot toasted bread to cool slightly.
> Top with 4 pieces of cucumber and an even amount of pickles. Place an even amount of brisket on top of the pickles. Add 2 to 3 sprigs of cilantro on top of the beef and your desired amount of jalapenos.
> Top with the other piece of baguette and serve immediately.

# Roast Beef Bánh Mì

You'll never want another roast beef sandwich after trying this. The mayonnaise has been switched out for a horseradish aioli, and topped with a honey lime jalapeno vinaigrette. It's spicy delicious!

Prep Time: 20 Minutes
Cook Time: 2 Minutes
Servings: 4

## INGREDIENTS:
*Aioli:*
1 teaspoon fresh horseradish
1 cup mayonnaise
2 tablespoon lemon juice
2 garlic cloves, minced
salt and pepper to taste

*Vinaigrette:*
2 tablespoons lime juice
2 tablespoons apple cider vinegar
2 tablespoons honey
1/4 cup light flavored olive oil
1/4 teaspoon kosher salt
2-4 small jalapeño peppers halved with stem and seeds removed

1 pound thinly sliced roast beef
1 pound mix of pickled daikon radish and carrots
8-12 sprigs of cilantro
16 thinly sliced cucumbers strips or spears
4 7-inch Vietnamese baguettes

## DIRECTIONS:

> Whisk together the aioli ingredients. Place all the vinaigrette ingredients in a blender or food processor and blend until smooth.
> Cut the baguettes lengthwise and spread aioli on the cut side of each piece. Place them in the oven for a couple minutes. Allow the hot toasted bread to cool slightly.
> Top with 4 pieces of cucumber and an even amount of pickles. Place an even amount of roast beef on top of the pickles. Add 2 to 3 sprigs of cilantro on top of the beef and drizzle with the vinaigrette.
> Top with the other piece of baguette and serve immediately.

# Red Curry Ground Beef Bánh Mì

Think of this as an Asian style sloppy joe. The curry is both creamy and spicy and goes so well with the pickles!

Prep Time: 10 Minutes
Cook Time: 20 Minutes
Servings: 4

## INGREDIENTS:
*Red Curry:*
*3 tablespoons extra-virgin olive oil*
*1/4 cup minced shallot*
*2 garlic cloves, minced*
*2 to 3 tablespoons red curry paste*
*1 pound ground beef*
*About 1/4 teaspoon kosher salt*
*1 cup canned coconut milk*
*2 teaspoons lime juice*

*1 pound mix of pickled daikon radish and carrots*
*8-12 sprigs of cilantro*
*16 thinly sliced cucumbers strips or spears*
*Thinly sliced jalapenos if you want more heat*
*4 7-inch Vietnamese baguettes*

## DIRECTIONS:
❯ Put 1 tablespoon of oil in a big frying pan and heat on medium heat. Put in the garlic and shallots and allow the mixture to cook until the shallots soften, around 3 minutes. Mix in the curry paste, and stir the mixture for 45 seconds. Put in the salt and ground beef and break the beef into small chunks. Cook until the meat is just cooked, around 5 minutes, stirring occasionally.

> Lower the temperature to medium low and put in the coconut milk, stir occasionally, and let the milk absorb into the sauce, around 8 minutes. Then stir in the lime juice.
> Cut the baguettes lengthwise and spread some curry on the cut side of each piece. Place them in the oven for a couple minutes. Allow the hot toasted bread to cool slightly.
> Top with 4 pieces of cucumber and an even amount of pickles. Place an even amount of ground beef on top of the pickles. Add 2 to 3 sprigs of cilantro on top of the beef and drizzle with curry.
> Top with the other piece of baguette and serve immediately.

# Poultry

---

## Banh Ga Nuong

---

This classic features marinated chicken that's been spiced with 5 spice powder, and garlic. 5 spice is packed with a spicy, sweet flavor that goes well with the aromatic flavor of the garlic and the tangy flavor of the pickles.

Prep Time: 25 Minutes
Cook Time: 30 Minutes
Servings: 4

## INGREDIENTS:

*Chicken:*
*6 Chicken Thighs,* bone in and skin on
*1 Tablespoon Five-Spice Powder*
*¼ Cup Granulated Sugar*
*2 Teaspoons Black Pepper*
*3 Tablespoons Minced Garlic*
*2 Tablespoons Vegetable Oil*
*½ Cup Maggi Seasoning Sauce*

*1 pound mix of pickled daikon radish and carrots*
*8-12 sprigs of cilantro*
*16 thinly sliced cucumber strips or spears*
*4 7-inch Vietnamese baguettes*
*1 jar mayonnaise*
*A few thinly sliced jalapenos, to taste*

## DIRECTIONS:

> Whisk together the dry chicken spices in a large bowl. Then mix in the oil, sauce, and garlic. Stir until the spices dissolve. Place the bowl in the refrigerator, covered for 1 hour.
> Preheat your oven to 400F.
> Place the chicken skin side up on a baking sheet that's been greased. Cook in the oven for about 30 minutes, until cooked through. Place the cooked chicken in a plate. When it's cool enough to handle, remove the skin and bones, and shred the meat.
> Cut the baguettes lengthwise and spread mayonnaise on the cut side of each piece. Place them in the oven for a couple minutes. Allow the hot toasted bread to cool slightly.
> Top with 4 pieces of cucumber and an even amount of pickles. Place an even amount of chicken on top of the pickles. Add 2 to 3 sprigs of cilantro on top with your desired amount of jalapenos.
> Top with the other piece of baguette and serve immediately.

# Thanksgiving Turkey Bánh Mì

This is a great way to use your leftovers for thanksgiving or have a taste of thanksgiving any time of year. We use a cranberry aioli to get things started, and top the sandwich with pickled green beans.

Prep Time:  15 Minutes
Cook Time: 2 Minutes
Servings: 4

## INGREDIENTS:
*Aioli:*
*½ cup cranberry sauce, either whole berry or jellied*
*½ cup mayonnaise*
*1 teaspoon Dijon mustard*
*1 clove garlic, minced*

*1 pound thinly sliced roast turkey*
*1 pound pickled green beans*
*8-12 sprigs of mint*
*16 thinly sliced cucumbers strips or spears*
*Slivered almonds*
*4 7-inch Vietnamese baguettes*
*Sliced Jalapenos if you want some heat*

## DIRECTIONS:
➤ Whisk together the aioli ingredients.
➤ Cut the baguettes lengthwise and spread aioli on the cut side of each piece. Place them in the oven for a couple minutes. Allow the hot toasted bread to cool slightly.
➤ Top with 4 pieces of cucumber and an even amount of pickles. Sprinkle some almonds on the pickles. Place an even amount of roast

turkey on top of the pickles and almonds. Add 2 to 3 sprigs of mint on top of the turkey and top with jalapenos if using.

> Top with the other piece of baguette and serve immediately.

# Southwestern Turkey Bánh Mì

This has all the heat and flavor of the southwest. It starts with a chipotle aioli, and gets more flavor from the hatch chilies, before finishing off with some creamy heat from the avocado jalapeno dressing.

Prep Time:  15 Minutes
Cook Time: 2 Minutes
Servings: 4

## INGREDIENTS:
*Aioli:*
*1/2 cup mayonnaise*
*1/4 cup sour cream*
*2 chipotle chilies from 1 can of chipotles in adobo*
*2 tablespoon freshly squeezed lime juice*

*Dressing:*
*1 avocado, pitted and skinned*
*1 cup water*
*juice from ½ lime*
*1 garlic clove*
*1 jalapeno pepper, de-seeded*
*1 tablespoon agave nectar*
*1 pinch salt*

*1 pound thinly sliced roast turkey*
*1 pound mix of pickled daikon radish and carrots*
*8-12 sprigs of cilantro*
*16 thinly sliced cucumbers strips or spears*
*A few fresh hatch chilies or canned hatch chilies, chopped*
*4 7-inch Vietnamese baguettes*

## DIRECTIONS:

> Put the aioli ingredients in a blender or food processor and blend until smooth.
> Place all the dressing ingredients in a blender or food processor and blend until smooth.
> Cut the baguettes lengthwise and spread aioli on the cut side of each piece. Place them in the oven for a couple minutes. Allow the hot toasted bread to cool slightly.
> Top with 4 pieces of cucumber and an even amount of pickles. Place an even amount of roast turkey on top of the pickles. Add 2 to 3 sprigs of cilantro on top of the turkey and top with the hatch chilies. Drizzle with the avocado jalapeno dressing.
> Top with the other piece of baguette and serve immediately.

# Pesto Turkey Bánh Mì

The Bánh Mì is remade with a taste of Italy. You get a nice pesto aioli, which moves in a mix of pickled carrots and red bell pepper, and the sandwich is topped with pepperoncinis so you get that true Italian flavor.

Prep Time: 15 Minutes
Cook Time: 2 Minutes
Servings: 4

## INGREDIENTS:
*Aioli:*
*2 cups fresh basil leaves*
*1 cup mayonnaise*
*½ cup grated Parmesan cheese*
*¼ cup toasted pine nuts*
*3 cloves garlic*
*2 tablespoons fresh lemon juice*
*¼ teaspoon salt*

*1 pound thinly sliced roast turkey*
*1 pound mix of pickled red bell pepper and carrots*
*8-12 sprigs of basil*
*16 thinly sliced cucumbers strips or spears*
*A few pepperoncinis, thinly sliced*
*4 7-inch Vietnamese baguettes*

## DIRECTIONS:
> Put the aioli ingredients in a blender or food processor and blend until smooth.
> Cut the baguettes lengthwise and spread aioli on the cut side of each piece. Place them in the oven for a couple minutes. Allow the hot toasted bread to cool slightly.

> Top with 4 pieces of cucumber and an even amount of pickles. Place an even amount of roast turkey on top of the pickles. Add 2 to 3 sprigs of basil on top of the turkey and top with the pepperoncinis.
> Top with the other piece of baguette and serve immediately.

# Spicy Crispy Chicken Bánh Mì

This Bánh Mì features delicious crispy chicken that's been marinated in delicious Asian spices. The sandwich gets some nice heat from the Sriracha mayo.

Prep Time:  15 Minutes
Cook Time: 12 Minutes
Servings: 4

## INGREDIENTS:
1/2 cup fish sauce
1 tablespoon sugar
1 tablespoon Sriracha
2 tablespoons fresh-squeezed lime juice
2 tablespoons sesame oil
1 tablespoon ginger, grated
2 garlic cloves, grated
2 chicken breasts

### Mayo:
1/2 cup mayo
1 tablespoon Sriracha
1 tablespoon fresh-squeezed lime juice

1 pound thinly sliced roast turkey
1 pound mix of daikon radish and carrots
8-12 sprigs of cilantro
16 thinly sliced cucumbers strips or spears
A few thinly sliced jalapenos, to taste
4 7-inch Vietnamese baguettes

## DIRECTIONS:

> Mix the first 5 ingredients in a bowl then mix in the ginger and cloves. Slice the chicken against the grain and put it in the mixture. Place the mixture in refrigerator for at least an hour, covered.
> Heat a tablespoon of oil in a wok on medium-high heat. Stir-fry the chicken in 2 batches. Cook each batch for 4-5 minutes, until it's crispy
> Mix all the mayo ingredients together in a bowl.
> Cut the baguettes lengthwise and spread aioli on the cut side of each piece. Place them in the oven for a couple minutes. Allow the hot toasted bread to cool slightly.
> Top with 4 pieces of cucumber and an even amount of pickles. Place an even amount of chicken on top of the pickles. Add 2 to 3 sprigs of cilantro on top of the chicken and top with the jalapenos.
> Top with the other piece of baguette and serve immediately.

# Vegetarian

## Bánh Mì Chay

This is an easy vegetarian version of the sandwich. It features marinated tofu that does a great job of providing flavor thanks to the soy sauce, paprika, lime, and maple syrup.

Prep Time: 20 Minutes
Cook Time: 13 Minutes
Servings: 4

## INGREDIENTS:

*Tofu:*
1 block extra-firm tofu, drained
3 tablespoons lime juice
2 tablespoons soy sauce, tamari, or coconut aminos
2 tablespoons maple syrup
1 clove garlic, minced
1 tablespoon smoked paprika

2 tablespoons peanut oil
1 pound mix of pickled daikon radish and carrots
8-12 sprigs of cilantro
16 thinly sliced cucumber strips or spears
4 7-inch Vietnamese baguettes
1 jar mayonnaise
A few thinly sliced jalapenos, to taste

## DIRECTIONS:

> Mix together all of the seasoning for the tofu in a bowl. Once mixed add the tofu. Cover the bowl and refrigerate for at least an hour
> Heat the peanut oil in a pan on medium-high heat. Add in the tofu and allow it to cook for 6 to 7 until it starts get golden on the sides. Flip the tofu and cook for another 4 minute.
> Cut the tofu in to 4 equal portions.
> Cut the baguettes lengthwise and spread mayonnaise on the cut side of each piece. Place them in the oven for a couple minutes. Allow the hot toasted bread to cool slightly.
> Top with 4 pieces of cucumber and an even amount of pickles. Place one of the portions of tofu on top of the pickles. Add 2 to 3 sprigs of cilantro on top with your desired amount of jalapenos.
> Top with the other piece of baguette and serve immediately.

# Vegan Beef Lemongrass Bánh Mì

This is an easy way for vegans to get a meaty sandwich. Seitan has a meat like texture and is flavored perfectly with the lemongrass.

Prep Time: 20 Minutes
Cook Time: 15 Minutes
Servings: 4

## INGREDIENTS:

*Seitan:*
20 ounces seitan
3 tablespoon oil
1 large shallot or 3 small shallots, finely diced
4-5 cloves garlic (1 heaping tablespoon of minced garlic)
1/3 cup shredded lemongrass (about 1-2 stalks)
3-4 tablespoon soy sauce (to taste)
Black pepper to taste

2 tablespoons peanut oil
1 pound mix of pickled daikon radish and carrots
8-12 sprigs of cilantro
16 thinly sliced cucumber strips or spears
4 7-inch Vietnamese baguettes
1 jar vegan mayonnaise
A few thinly sliced jalapenos, to taste

## DIRECTIONS:

> Heat the oil in a pan on medium-high heat. Add in the shallots and allow them to cook until translucent, about 5 minutes. Mix in the garlic and allow it to get fragrant, about 30 seconds. Add the lemongrass and cook for another 1-2 minutes, until fragrant.

> Mix in the seitan and get it well coated with the herbs. Pour in the soy sauce and allow the seitan to cook until it turns brown, about 5 minutes. If the seitan starts to dry out add a little water.
> Cut the baguettes lengthwise and spread mayonnaise on the cut side of each piece. Place them in the oven for a couple minutes. Allow the hot toasted bread to cool slightly.
> Top with 4 pieces of cucumber and an even amount of pickles. Place an equal amount of seitan on top of the pickles. Add 2 to 3 sprigs of cilantro on top with your desired amount of jalapenos.
> Top with the other piece of baguette and serve immediately.

# Spicy Ginger Eggplant Bánh Mì

Eggplant makes a great stand in for meat because it's thick and has a meaty texture. The ginger marinade for the eggplant is the perfect complement for the garlic ginger aioli and tart pickles.

Prep Time: 20 Minutes
Cook Time: 15 Minutes
Servings: 4

## INGREDIENTS:
### Aioli:
2 cups mayonnaise
1 piece fresh ginger, peeled and grated
2 garlic cloves, pressed
2 teaspoons fresh lemon juice
1 dash cayenne pepper
1/4 cup dry breadcrumbs


### Eggplant:
1 large eggplant, sliced lengthwise into 4 thick pieces, about 1 inch thick
3 tablespoons soy sauce
3 tablespoons rice wine vinegar
2 tablespoons agave, or other sweetener
1 inch ginger, peeled and minced
1 clove garlic, minced
1 Tablespoon Sriracha or chili paste
1 Tablespoon vegetable oil
pepper to taste

1 pound mix of pickled daikon radish and carrots

*8-12 sprigs of cilantro*
*16 thinly sliced cucumber strips or spears*
*4 7-inch Vietnamese baguettes*
*A few thinly sliced jalapenos, to taste*

## DIRECTIONS:

> Preheat your oven to 400F.
> Whisk together all the eggplant ingredients except for the eggplant in a bowl. Place the eggplant in the mixture. Place the eggplant on a baking sheets that's been lined with parchment paper. Drizzle more of the marinade on both sides of the eggplant so it's well covered. Cook in the oven for about 15 minutes, until the eggplant is brown. Flip the eggplant halfway through cooking.
> Place all the aioli ingredients in a blender or food processor and blend until smooth.
> Cut the baguettes lengthwise and spread aioli on the cut side of each piece. Place them in the oven for a couple minutes. Allow the hot toasted bread to cool slightly.
> Top with 4 pieces of cucumber and an even amount of pickles. Place an equal amount of eggplant on top of the pickles. Add 2 to 3 sprigs of cilantro on top with your desired amount of jalapenos.
> Top with the other piece of baguette and serve immediately.

# Ginger Lemongrass Portobello Mushroom Bánh Mì

The lemongrass and ginger mix together to create a spicy and aromatic flavor. The mushroom soaks up all the delicious flavor, and get some heat from the Sriracha mayo. You can easily make this vegan friendly with the use of vegan mayo.

Prep Time: 1 Hour 15 Minutes
Cook Time: 10 Minutes
Servings: 4

## INGREDIENTS:
*Mayo:*
*1/2 cup mayo or vegan mayo*
*1 tablespoon Sriracha*
*1 tablespoon fresh-squeezed lime juice*

*Mushrooms:*
*18 ounces Portobello mushrooms stalks trimmed*
*4 tablespoons soy sauce*
*1 1/2 tablespoons honey*
*1 teaspoon ginger grated*
*1 1/2 tsp lemongrass white part only, grated*
*2 tablespoons olive oil*

*1 pound mix of pickled daikon radish and carrots*
*8-12 sprigs of cilantro*
*16 thinly sliced cucumber strips or spears*
*4 7-inch Vietnamese baguettes*
*A few thinly sliced jalapenos, to taste*

## DIRECTIONS:

> Whisk together the soy sauce, honey, ginger, and lemongrass in a bowl. Slice the mushrooms into 1 inch pieces, and put them in the marinade bowl. Mix everything together until the mushrooms are well coated. Place the bowl in the refrigerated, covered, for at least an hour.

> Place half the olive oil in a large frying pan and heat on medium-high heat. Add in half the mushrooms and allow them to cook for 2-3 minute before flipping them and cooking for an additional 2 minutes. Repeat the process with the other half of the mushrooms and oil.

> Whisk all of the mayo ingredients together until well combined.

> Cut the baguettes lengthwise and spread mayo on the cut side of each piece. Place them in the oven for a couple minutes. Allow the hot toasted bread to cool slightly.

> Top with 4 pieces of cucumber and an even amount of pickles. Place an equal amount of mushrooms on top of the pickles. Add 2 to 3 sprigs of cilantro on top with your desired amount of jalapenos.

> Top with the other piece of baguette and serve immediately.

# Grilled Vegetable Bánh Mì

This recipe is perfect for summer when it's grilling season. We use zucchini, bell peppers and eggplant, but feel free to swap in your favorite vegetables. The cilantro lime aioli gives a nice fresh flavor. Substitute vegan mayonnaise to make this recipe vegan.

Prep Time: 50 Minutes
Cook Time: 11 Minutes
Servings: 4

## INGREDIENTS:
*Mayo:*
1/3 cup fresh cilantro, chopped
1 lime, juice and zest of
1 -3 drop hot pepper sauce, depending on preference
1 teaspoon ground cumin
3/4 cup mayonnaise or vegan mayonnaise
1 large clove garlic

*Veggies:*
2 tbsp. toasted sesame oil
2 tbsp. rice wine vinegar
1 tbsp. tamari or soy sauce
1 clove garlic, minced
2 tbsp. thinly sliced green onions
1 1/4 lb. eggplant, zucchini, and bell pepper, or your favorite vegetables, cut into 1/4-inch slices
Salt and pepper to taste

1 pound mix of pickled daikon radish and carrots
8-12 sprigs of cilantro
16 thinly sliced cucumber strips or spears

*4 7-inch Vietnamese baguettes*
*A few thinly sliced jalapenos, to taste*

## DIRECTIONS:

> Whisk together the soy sauce, vinegar, sesame oil, and garlic in a big dish. Put the veggies and onions in the dish. Mix everything together until the veggies and onions are well coated. Place the bowl in the refrigerated, covered, for at least 30 minutes.

> Heat your grill to medium-high heat. Grill the veggies and onions for 5 minutes a side, until everything becomes tender. Make sure you baste the veggies with the marinade throughout the grilling process. Salt and pepper the veggies to taste when cooked.

> Place all the aioli ingredients in a blender or food processor and blend until smooth.

> Cut the baguettes lengthwise and spread aioli on the cut side of each piece. Place them in the oven for a couple minutes. Allow the hot toasted bread to cool slightly.

> Top with 4 pieces of cucumber and an even amount of pickles. Place an equal amount of veggies on top of the pickles. Add 2 to 3 sprigs of cilantro on top with your desired amount of jalapenos.

> Top with the other piece of baguette and serve immediately.

# Fish

## Bánh Mì Ca Moi

This is a classic Bánh Mì that uses sardines. The sardines are warmed up with a little fish sauce to add flavor and topped with a delicious Vietnamese tomato sauce. It's a refreshing way to eat fish. They're perfect for picnics.

Prep Time: 20 Minutes
Cook Time: 15 Minutes
Servings: 4

## INGREDIENTS:

*Sauce:*
½ cup water
½ tablespoon cornstarch
½ tablespoon sugar
½ tablespoon soy sauce
½ teaspoon salt
8 ounces canned tomato sauce
1 tablespoons canola oil
1 cloves garlic, minced
½ tablespoon sugar
1 scallion, chopped
½ teaspoon black pepper
Light sprinkling of garlic powder
Light sprinkling of onion powder
Light sprinkling of ginger powder

3 - 5½ ounce cans of sardines in tomato sauce
1 teaspoon fish sauce

*1 pound mix of pickled daikon radish and carrots*
*8-12 sprigs of cilantro*
*16 thinly sliced cucumber strips or spears*
*4 7-inch Vietnamese baguettes*
*1 jar mayonnaise*
*A few thinly sliced jalapenos, to taste*

## DIRECTIONS:

> Mix together the tomato sauce, corn starch, water, sugar, soy sauce, and salt.
> Heat the oil in a small saucepan on high heat. Put in the garlic and allow it to cook for 30 seconds. Add in the corn starch mixture and stir everything until the sauce thickens.
> Heat a small saucepan on medium heat. Add in the sardines and fish sauce. Cook for a few minutes until the sardines have warmed up and absorbed the fish sauce.
> Cut the baguettes lengthwise and spread mayonnaise on the cut side of each piece. Place them in the oven for a couple minutes. Allow the hot toasted bread to cool slightly.
> Place the sardines on the bottom piece of baguette. Drizzle with the tomato sauce. Top with 4 cucumbers an even amount of pickles. Add 2 to 3 sprigs of cilantro on top with your desired amount of jalapenos.
> Top with the other piece of baguette and serve immediately.

# Salmon Bánh Mì

The salmon has a nice mix of sweet, spicy, and savory thanks to the brown sugar, fish sauce and Sriracha. The aioli adds freshness from the lemon and ginger.

Prep Time: 1 Hour 15 Minutes
Cook Time: 8 Minutes
Servings: 4

## INGREDIENTS:
*Aioli:*
*2 cups mayonnaise*
*1 piece fresh ginger, peeled and grated*
*2 garlic cloves, pressed*
*1 tablespoon fresh lemon juice*
*1 dash cayenne pepper*
*1/4 cup dry breadcrumbs*

*Salmon:*
*1/4 cup boiling water*
*1/4 cup lightly packed brown sugar*
*1 tablespoon Sriracha chili sauce*
*1/4 cup fish sauce*
*1 teaspoon low-sodium tamari*
*3 cloves garlic, finely minced*
*16 ounces skinless wild salmon fillet (preferably thin), pin bones removed,*

*1 pound mix of pickled daikon radish and carrots*
*8-12 sprigs of cilantro*
*16 thinly sliced cucumber strips or spears*
*4 7-inch Vietnamese baguettes*

*A few thinly sliced jalapenos, to taste*

## DIRECTIONS:

> Whisk Boiling water and sugar together until the sugar completely dissolves. Mix in the tamari, fish sauce, garlic, and Sriracha. Reserve 3 tablespoons of the mixture as a sauce for the sandwich. Allow the mixture to cool down to room temperature and then place it in a shallow baking dish. Add in the salmon and coat it with the marinade. Cover the dish and place it in the refrigerator for 1 hour. Flip the salmon after 30 minutes.

> Preheat your broiler.

> Put the salmon in a shallow baking dish and place the dish 6 inches from your broiler. Let the salmon cook for around 6-8 minutes, until it turns gold brown. The salmon may be cooked faster if you're using thinner pieces.

> Place all the aioli ingredients in a blender or food processor and blend until smooth.

> Cut the baguettes lengthwise and spread aioli on the cut side of each piece. Place them in the oven for a couple minutes. Allow the hot toasted bread to cool slightly.

> Top with 4 pieces of cucumber and an even amount of pickles. Place an equal amount of salmon on top of the pickles. Add 2 to 3 sprigs of cilantro on top with your desired amount of jalapenos and drizzle with the reserved sauce.

> Top with the other piece of baguette and serve immediately.

# Soft Shell Crab Bánh Mì

Soft shell crab is a seasonal treat that is unbelievable delicious. We fry them to perfection and then add some spicy ginger aioli for a nice kick. Make sure you have the crabs cleaned wherever you buy them so you don't have to worry about it.

Prep Time: 20 Minutes
Cook Time: 6 Minutes
Servings: 4

## INGREDIENTS:
*Aioli:*
*½ cup mayonnaise*
*3 tablespoons Sambal Oelek, Sriracha, or other chili paste*
*1, 2-inch piece fresh peeled ginger, chopped*
*2 medium garlic cloves, chopped*

## Crab:
*4 large soft-shell crabs, cleaned*
*1/2 cup cornstarch*
*Pinch of salt*
*3 tablespoons vegetable oil*

*1 pound mix of pickled daikon radish and carrots*
*8-12 sprigs of cilantro*
*16 thinly sliced cucumber strips or spears*
*4 7-inch Vietnamese baguettes*
*A few thinly sliced jalapenos, to taste*

## DIRECTIONS:
> Mix together the cornstarch and salt in a shallow bowl. Lightly coat the crab with the cornstarch mixture.

> Heat the oil in large skillet on medium-high heat until it shimmers. Place the crabs with the shell side down into the skillet and cook for 3 minutes. Flip the crabs for another 3 minutes. They should be a beautiful golden brown when cooked. Place the cooked crabs on a plate lined with paper towels.

> Place all the aioli ingredients in a blender or food processor and blend until smooth.

> Cut the baguettes lengthwise and spread aioli on the cut side of each piece. Place them in the oven for a couple minutes. Allow the hot toasted bread to cool slightly.

> Top with 4 pieces of cucumber and an even amount of pickles. Place one crab on top of the pickles. Add 2 to 3 sprigs of cilantro on top with your desired amount of jalapenos.

> Top with the other piece of baguette and serve immediately.

# Fried Oyster Bánh Mì

This is a mashup of New Orleans and Vietnamese cuisine. The oysters are breaded in cornmeal and fried like you would for a Po' Boy in New Orleans. It's got a spicy aioli that fits both New Orleans and Vietnamese cuisine.

Prep Time: 20 Minutes
Cook Time: 16 Minutes
Servings: 4

## INGREDIENTS:
*Aioli:*
*2 green onions, finely chopped*
*2/3 cup mayonnaise*
*1 tbsp. Sriracha*
*Salt and pepper to taste*

## Oysters:
*2 cups peanut oil or frying oil*
*16 jarred small oysters or fresh shucked oysters*
*1 cup flour*
*2 eggs, beaten*
*1 cup cornmeal*
*4 (8- inch) sections crusty baguettes*
*2 jalapenos, sliced*
*16 sprigs cilantro*

*1 pound mix of pickled daikon radish and carrots*
*8-12 sprigs of cilantro*
*16 thinly sliced cucumber strips or spears*
*4 7-inch Vietnamese baguettes*
*A few thinly sliced jalapenos, to taste*

## DIRECTIONS:

> Heat the peanut oil to 375F in a big pan.
> Setup 3 bowls, 1 with the flour, 1 with the egg, and 1 with the cornmeal. Coat the oysters with the flour, then egg, and finally the cornmeal.
> Place the oysters in the pan in batches of 4 and cook until golden brown, around 4 minutes. Place the cooked oysters on a plate lined with paper towels
> Place all the aioli ingredients in a blender or food processor and blend until smooth.
> Cut the baguettes lengthwise and spread aioli on the cut side of each piece. Place them in the oven for a couple minutes. Allow the hot toasted bread to cool slightly.
> Top with 4 pieces of cucumber and an even amount of pickles. Place an equal amount of oysters on top of the pickles. Add 2 to 3 sprigs of cilantro on top with your desired amount of jalapenos.
> Top with the other piece of baguette and serve immediately.

# Coconut Shrimp Bánh Mì

The shrimp is so sweet and tropical thanks to the coconut. The basil lime aioli adds freshness and aromatic flavor that balances the sweetness of the shrimp with the tanginess of the pickles.

Prep Time: 20 Minutes
Cook Time: 5 Minutes
Servings: 4

## INGREDIENTS:

*Aioli:*
*1 garlic clove, peeled and minced*
*1 lime, zested*
*8-10 basil leaves, cut into thin strips*
*1 cup mayonnaise*

## Shrimp:

*1/2 cup rice flour*
*1/2 cup unsweetened shredded coconut*
*1 pound shrimp cleaned, deveined, tails removed*
*1 tablespoon olive oil*
*Juice of 1 lime*
*sea salt and freshly ground black pepper, to taste*

*1 pound mix of pickled daikon radish and carrots*
*8-12 sprigs of cilantro*
*16 thinly sliced cucumber strips or spears*
*4 7-inch Vietnamese baguettes*
*A few thinly sliced jalapenos, to taste*

## DIRECTIONS:

> Whisk together the rice flour and coconut in a medium bowl.

> Coat the shrimp with the lime juice and then coat it with the flour mixture.
> Heat the olive oil on medium heat in a medium cast iron skillet. Add in the shrimp and cook for around 2 minutes, until golden brown. Flip the shrimp. Cook for an additional minute.
> Place all the aioli ingredients in a blender or food processor and blend until smooth.
> Cut the baguettes lengthwise and spread aioli on the cut side of each piece. Place them in the oven for a couple minutes. Allow the hot toasted bread to cool slightly.
> Top with 4 pieces of cucumber and an even amount of pickles. Place an equal amount of shrimp on top of the pickles. Add 2 to 3 sprigs of cilantro on top with your desired amount of jalapenos.
> Top with the other piece of baguette and serve immediately.

# Lobster Roll Bánh Mì

People in Maine might be a little angry about this sandwich but it's delicious. The lobster is tossed in a refreshing dressing that has creamy coconut milk, fish sauce, and mint.

Prep Time: 20 Minutes
Cook Time: 5 Minutes
Servings: 4

## INGREDIENTS:

*Dressing:*
*1 Cup Coconut Milk*
*1/2 Cup Mayo*
*1/4 Cup Fish Sauce*
*1/2 Cup Mint Chopped*

*4 cups of cooked lobster*
*1 pound mix of pickled daikon radish and carrots*
*8-12 sprigs of cilantro*
*16 thinly sliced cucumber strips or spears*
*4 7-inch Vietnamese baguettes*
*A few thinly sliced jalapenos, to taste*

## DIRECTIONS:

> Whisk together all of the dressing ingredients until well combined.
> Place the lobster in a bowl and pour half of the dressing in the bowl. Mix together until the lobster is well coated with the dressing. If that's not enough dressing slowly pours in and mix until coated. You want the lobster to have a light coat of dressing on it.
> Cut the baguettes lengthwise and spread some of the dressing on the cut side of each piece. Place them in the oven for a couple minutes. Allow the hot toasted bread to cool slightly.

> Top with 4 pieces of cucumber and an even amount of pickles. Place an equal amount of lobster on top of the pickles. Add 2 to 3 sprigs of cilantro on top with your desired amount of jalapenos.
> Top with the other piece of baguette and serve immediately.

# Next on The List!

## Here's What You Do Now...

>>> IF YOU LIKE THE BOOK...GIVE US A COOL REVIEW! :) <<<

**If you were pleased with our book then PLEASE LEAVE US A COOL REVIEW ON AMAZON where you purchased this book!** In the world of an author who writes books independently, your reviews are not only touching but important so that we know you like the material we have prepared for "you" our audience! So, leave us a review...we would love to see that you enjoyed our book!

If for any reason that you were less than happy with your experience then send me an email at **Info@RecipeNerds.com** and let me know how we can better your experience. We always come out with a few volumes of our books and will possibly be able to address some of your concerns. Do keep in mind that we strive to do our best to give you the highest quality of what "we the independent authors" pour our heart and tears into.

Thank you for your purchase. I am very excited to show you the art and craft of making Bánh Mì style sandwiches from your home! Hope you enjoy and learn many new Vietnamese sandwich making techniques! Yours Truly, Nancy Nguyen

## Yours to Keep!

# GET YOUR FREE GUIDE TODAY!

**Steps to Making the Perfect Home Made Vietnamese Craft Bánh Mì Sandwich!** This quick start guide will show you the way to get the **BEST** Bánh Mì sandwich made fast! This **QUICK STEP GUIDE** will make you a pro at crafting those sandwich, and your friends and family will love you for it! Simply click the button below! Enjoy your Bánh Mì Vietnamese Sandwich Experience! **GET YOURS NOW!**

http://eepurl.com/dvHwST

# About the Author

Nancy Nguyen is a Vietnamese chef that has migrate into the US at an early age. She has always been a lover of creating food for others to enjoy. She is a self-made personal chef and travels back to her home country to visit family and get new ideas to further accelerate her career as a chef. Nancy has always been a creator of food and now has enjoyed putting this beautiful book together to share with you.

I hope you enjoyed this personal handbook guide to creating our famous Vietnamese Banh Mi sandwiches. I am creating more books to share with you so just look out for my publications!

*And remember, leave me a cool review on Amazon!

Love, Peace and Happiness!
Nancy Nguyen!

# Personal Bánh Mì Recipes & Notes:

**Create your very own "Marvelous Masterpieces".** Log them in this section. You will be amazed on how many ideas you come up with! **Now get creating!**

| Bánh Mì Name | Meat | Bread | Bánh Mì Toppings |
|---|---|---|---|
| | | | |
| | | | |
| | | | |
| | | | |
| | | | |
| | | | |
| | | | |
| | | | |
| | | | |
| | | | |
| | | | |
| | | | |
| | | | |
| | | | |
| | | | |
| | | | |
| | | | |
| | | | |
| | | | |
| | | | |
| | | | |
| | | | |

Nancy Nguyen

Made in the USA
Middletown, DE
28 November 2021

53606333R00047